Types of Appliqués

Blindstitched appliqué resembles traditional hand stitching but is sewn with the machine blindstitch.

Frayed appliqué is a contemporary style with exposed raw edges.

Satin-stitched appliqué, sewn with machine satin stitching, has more defined edges.

✂ Cutting Directions

Cut five 7" × 9" (18 × 23 cm) rectangles from fabric background.

For tulips on two quilt blocks, use the patterns on page 3 to make cardboard templates for the tulip flower and tulip leaf. Cut six flowers and six leaves from fabric as on page 5, step 1; turn the template over to cut two of the leaves. Cut six stems from bias tape to desired lengths. Three leaves, three flowers, and three stems are used for each quilt block.

For geraniums on two quilt blocks, cut six leaves and 16 to 20 florets, using the patterns on page 3. Cut two fabric stems 1/4" × 3" (6 mm × 7.5 cm). Three leaves, eight to ten florets, and one stem are used for each quilt block.

For hibiscus on one quilt block, cut two flowers and two leaves, using the patterns on page 3; turn the pattern over to cut one of the leaves.

YOU WILL NEED

3/8 **yd. (0.35 m) fabric** for background.

3/4 **yd. (0.7 m) fabric** for 1 1/2" (3.8 cm) border, backing, and binding.

Fabric scraps for flowers and leaves; double-fold bias tape for tulip stems.

Batting, about 13" × 35" (33 × 89 cm).

Cardboard, spray starch, and monofilament nylon thread for blindstitched appliqués.

3/4 **yd. (0.7 m) tear-away stabilizer.**

Patterns for the Garden Row Appliqué Sampler Quilt

TULIP LEAF

TULIP FLOWER

HIBISCUS FLOWER

GERANIUM FLORET

GERANIUM LEAF

HIBISCUS LEAF

How to Make a Garden Row Appliqué Sampler Quilt

1) Follow steps 2 to 5 on page 5 for the blindstitched appliqués, arranging pieces for three tulips on quilt block as shown; place bottom of leaves at raw edge of block. For stems, trim away one folded edge of bias tape to reduce bulk. Repeat for second quilt block.

2) Follow steps 1 to 7 on page 6 for the frayed appliqués, arranging pieces for one geranium on quilt block as shown. Repeat for second quilt block.

3) Follow steps 1 to 4 on page 7 for the satin-stitched appliqués, arranging pieces for two hibiscus flowers on quilt block as shown.

4) Stitch stamens on hibiscus, using free-motion sewing.

5) Stitch blocks together in ¼" (6 mm) seams, as shown. Press the quilt top, taking care not to overpress appliqués.

6) Cut and attach border strips; cut width of border strips is 2" (5 cm). Cut backing 13" × 35" (33 × 89 cm); layer and baste the quilt top, batting, and backing.

7) Quilt, using stitch-in-the-ditch method, along the seamlines. Quilt around flowers. If desired, quilt along design lines of hibiscus, to define petals. (Contrasting thread was used to show detail.)

8) Cut and apply binding; cut width of binding is 2" (5 cm). For wall hanging, attach fabric sleeve.

How to Sew a Blindstitched Appliqué

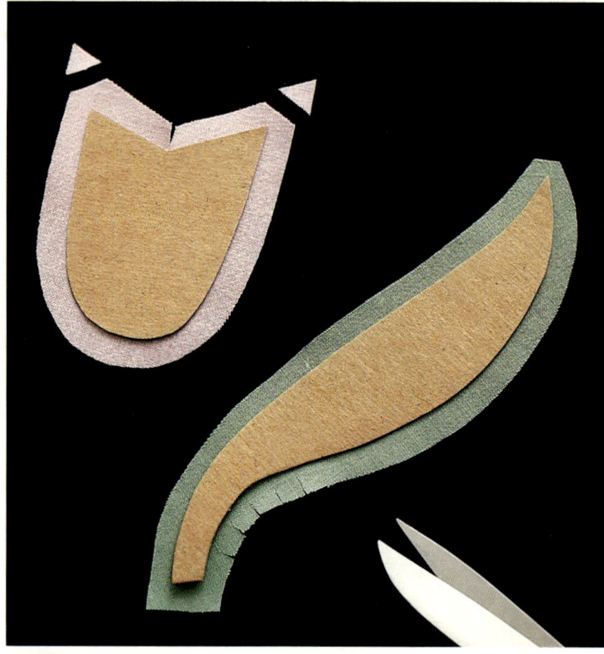

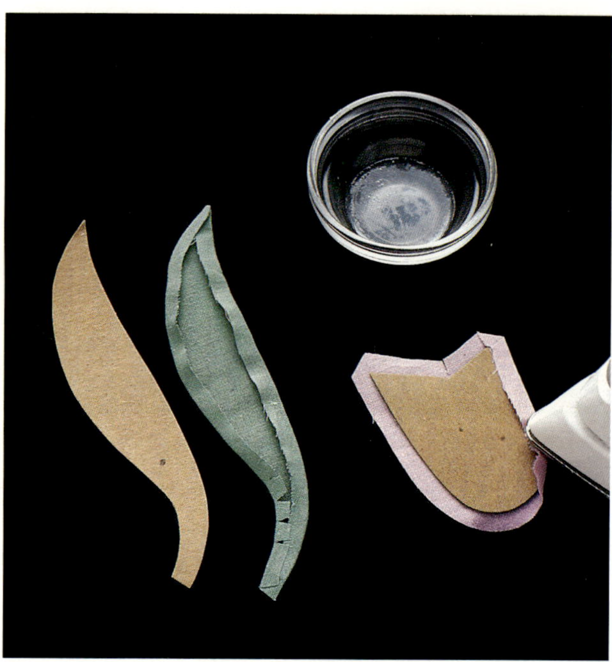

1) Cut cardboard templates to the *finished size* of appliqué pieces. Place template on fabric. Adding ¼" (6 mm) seam allowances, cut around template, using rotary cutter. Clip inside curves and corners almost to template; trim outside corners.

2) Spray starch in small bowl; dab starch on section of seam allowance. With tip of dry iron, press seam allowance over edge of template; press until spray starch dries. Continue pressing around the appliqué. Remove the template, and press appliqué, right side up.

3) Position appliqué design on the quilt block; mark the placement of the pieces, using chalk. Position tear-away stabilizer, cut larger than design, on wrong side of fabric. Pin or baste pieces in place; for layered design, apply first layer only.

4) Set machine for short blindstitch, with the stitch width about ¹⁄₁₆" (1.5 mm); use monofilament nylon thread in the needle. Blindstitch around pieces, catching edge with widest swing of stitch. (Contrasting thread was used to show detail.)

5) Pin or baste the second layer in place, and blindstitch. Repeat as necessary for any remaining layers. Remove tear-away stabilizer, taking care not to distort stitches.

How to Sew a Frayed Appliqué

1) Cut the appliqué pieces, using patterns; do not add seam allowances. Mark any design lines.

2) Position the appliqué design on quilt block; mark the placement of pieces, using chalk.

3) Glue-baste pieces in place ¼" (6 mm) from edges; for layered design, apply first layer only. Place tear-away stabilizer on wrong side of fabric.

4) Stitch around pieces, stitching ⅛" (3 mm) from raw edge; some designs may require free-motion sewing.

5) Glue-baste the second layer in place; stitch as in step 4. Repeat as necessary for any remaining layers.

6) Stitch on any design lines, using free-motion sewing, if necessary. Remove tear-away stabilizer, taking care not to distort stitches.

7) Brush edges of appliqué, if desired, using a stiff brush; this will ravel edges to add more texture.

How to Sew a Satin-stitched Appliqué

1) **Cut** appliqué pieces, using patterns; do not add seam allowances. Mark any design lines; patterns may be cut apart to serve as guide for marking.

2) **Position** pieces on quilt block; mark placement, using chalk. Position tear-away stabilizer on wrong side of fabric. Glue-baste or pin pieces in place; for layered design, apply first layer only.

3) **Set** machine for short, wide zigzag stitch; use machine embroidery thread in needle. Satin stitch around pieces; do not satin stitch edges that will be overlapped by other pieces. Add details, such as veins of leaves; for veins, use narrow zigzag stitch and taper ends.

4) **Glue-baste** second layer in place; satin stitch as in step 3. Repeat for any remaining layers. Remove the tear-away stabilizer, taking care not to distort stitches.

Satin-stitching Techniques for Appliqués

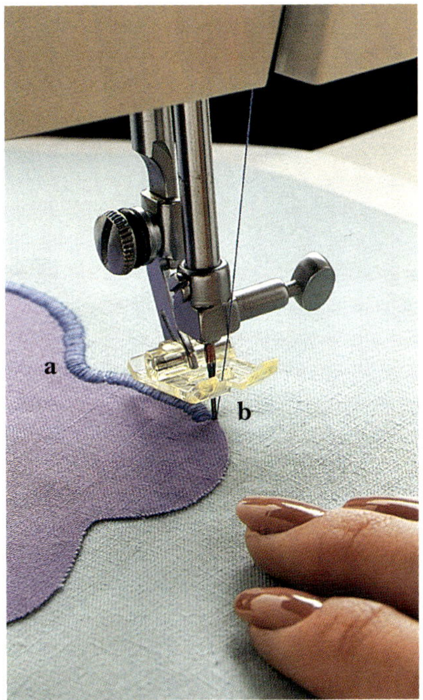

Curves. Pivot the fabric frequently, pivoting with the needle down. For inside curves, pivot with needle at inner edge of stitching (**a**); for outside curves, pivot with needle on outer edge of stitching (**b**).

Inside corners. Stitch past corner a distance equal to width of stitch, stopping with the needle down at the inner edge of stitching. Pivot fabric, and satin stitch next side of appliqué.

Outside corners. Stitch one stitch past edge of appliqué, stopping with needle down at outer edge of stitching. Pivot fabric, and satin stitch next side of appliqué.

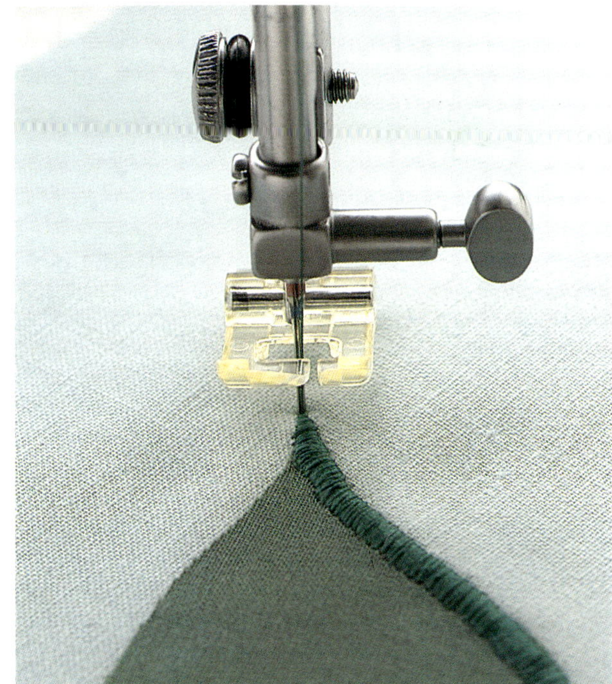

Points. 1) Stitch, stopping when inner edge of satin stitching meets the opposite side of the appliqué. Pivot the fabric slightly; continue stitching, gradually narrowing stitch width to 0 and stopping at point. (Presser foot was removed to show detail.)

2) Pivot fabric, and stitch back over previous stitches, gradually widening the stitch width to original width. Pivot fabric slightly, and stitch next side of appliqué.

Frayed appliqué and authentic African prints were used for the quilt above. Primitive figures were made from two fabric layers, the top layer cut smaller than the first.

More Appliqué Designs

The appliqué methods used for the Garden Row Appliqué Sampler Quilt can be used for many designs. Use the appliqué patterns available at quilt stores, or design your own appliqués, using books, cards, and artwork for design ideas.

Dancers

Finished size: 41" × 37½" (104 × 95.3 cm)

YOU WILL NEED

Solid red	1¼ yd. (1.15 m)
Solid green	⅓ yd. (0.32 m)
Solid gold	⅓ yd. (0.32 m)
Solid black	1¼ yd. (1.15 m)
"Lattice" print pane	⅝ yd. (0.6 m)
Bottom print strip	¼ yd. (0.25 m)
Backing	1¼ yd. (1.15 m)

✄ Cutting Directions

Cut gold, green, and red rectangles 8" × 15" (20.5 × 38 cm). Cut print panel 19" × 33" (48.5 × 84 cm). Cut red panel 22½" × 36½" (57.3 × 92.8 cm). Freehand-cut round corners and curved sides on all pieces. Cut bottom print strip 6¼" × 36¼" (15.7 × 92.1 cm). Cut black background to 41" × 37½" (104 × 95.3 cm).

Assembly Instructions

1) **Prepare** appliqués by cutting two figures for each panel, one trimmed ⅛" (3 mm) smaller than the underneath figure. Use each color once for the top figure and once for the underneath figure. Pin or glue-stick all panels and figures to black background as desired.

2) **Layer** backing, batting, and top, and baste together.

3) **Topstitch** ⅛" (3 mm) from the edges of all panels and top figures through all layers, using thread that matches fabric being sewn.

4) **Bind** edges of quilt and wash to fray edges, or use a stiff brush to fray edges.